MW00913180

5
Duties
As a
Christian
Citizen

BILL BRIGHT

Your 5 Duties As a Christian Citizen

Published by
New*Life* Publications
A ministry of Campus Crusade for Christ
P.O. Box 620877
Orlando, FL 32862-0877

Edited by Lynn Copeland

Design and typesetting by Genesis Group

Printed in the United States of America

ISBN 1-56399-135-7

Unless otherwise noted, Scripture references are from *The Living Bible,* © 1971 by Tyndale House Publishers, Wheaton, Illinois.

Scripture quotations designated NIV are from the *New International Version,* © 1973, 1978, 1984 by the International Bible Society. Published by Zondervan Bible Publishers, Grand Rapids, Michigan.

Scripture quotations designated NKJ are from the *New King James* version, © 1979, 1980, 1982 by Thomas Nelson Inc., Publishers, Nashville, Tennessee.

Contents

In selecting men for office, let principle be your guide. Regard not the particular sect or denomination of the candidate—look to his character... It is alleged by men of loose principles, or defective views of the subject, that religion and morality are not necessary or important qualifications for political stations. But the Scriptures teach a different doctrine. They direct that rulers should be men who rule in the fear of God, able men, such as fear God, men of truth, hating covetousness...

When a citizen gives his vote to a man of known immorality, he abuses his civic responsibility; he sacrifices not only his own interest, but that of his neighbor; he betrays the interest of his country.

—NOAH WEBSTER

Citizenship in a free country is a blessing from God. Our great system of self-government assures every Christian a voice in the affairs of the nation, and enables us to bring a heavenly perspective to the earthly realm. God wants us to do His will in government, just as in the church and in the home.

But too often we have disobeyed our Lord. We have ceased to be the "salt of the earth" and the "light of the world," as Christ has commanded us. As a result, the moral fiber of America is rotting away—and our priceless freedom is in grave jeopardy. Atheism is penetrating every area of our national life. America is faced with the greatest crisis in its history. We are in danger of losing our nation by default, and with it our individual freedoms and possibly our very lives.

If that should happen, our opportunity to help fulfill the Great Commission throughout the United States and the world will also be lost. And hundreds of millions will never have an opportunity to receive our Savior.

British statesman Edmund Burke said, "All that is necessary for the triumph of evil is for good men to do nothing." America is one of the last strongholds of freedom on earth—and citizens who are dedicated to God are the only resource for the preservation of our freedoms, including the freedom to serve Him.

It has been reliably estimated that more than half of the people of the United States profess faith in Jesus Christ. By following the simple guidelines contained in this booklet, even a small percentage of us can be used by God to set this nation on a new course of righteousness for His glory.

Charles Finney, who helped introduce half a million Americans to Christ, wrote in 1835:

"The time has come that Christians must vote for honest men and take consistent ground in politics, or the Lord will curse them...God cannot sustain this free and blessed country, which we love and pray for, unless the Church will take right ground. Politics are a part of religion in such a country as this, and Christians must do their duty to the country as a part of their duty to God...God will bless or curse this nation according to the course Christians take in politics."

His words are no less true for us today. Our nation's course is up to us.

Your Christian Citizen Checklist

Mark Twain understood the importance of a Christian's responsibility as a citizen. He wrote: "A Christian's first duty is to God. It then follows, as a matter of course, that it is his duty to carry his Christian code of morals to the polls and vote them...If Christians should vote their duty to God at the polls, they would carry every election, and do it with ease...it would bring about a moral revolution that would be incalculably beneficent. It would save the country."

With so much at stake in our nation, honestly answer these questions about your role:

☐ Do I pray faithfully for a spiritual revival to sweep America?

☐ Am I registered to vote? Do I encourage other Christians to register?

☐ Am I making a serious effort, along with my Christian friends, to become informed about the candidates and issues?

☐ Am I actively involved in helping to select and elect godly candidates to office?

☐ Do I vote in every election for the best candidates, regardless of party?

If you answered "no" to one or more of these questions, this booklet is "must" reading for you. It will bring you to a new realization that faith in our Lord implies obligation and duty to serve Him in all areas of life—including citizenship. And what is far more important, you will learn how to practice your citizenship for His glory.

God's Plan for a Nation's Leadership

To protect His people, God warns against ungodly leaders. The rule of the wicked is a direct violation of His will. "The wicked shall not rule the godly, lest the godly be forced to do wrong" (Psalm 125:3). Instead, God's plan is for us to have leaders who know Him and will rule according to His Word. "He who rules over men must be just, ruling in the fear of God" (2 Samuel 23:3, NKJ).

John Jay, first Chief Justice of the U.S. Supreme Court, was one of the three men most responsible for drafting the Constitution. In 1816 he wrote:

"Providence has given to our people the choice of their rulers, and it is the duty—as well as the

*privilege and interest—of our Christian nation to
select and prefer Christians for their rulers."*

Voting for and supporting moral candidates who support moral public policies is the minimum required of Christian citizens in a system of self-government. Godly people must vote for godly rulers. Christian lawyer Michael Whitehead put it this way: "If America is to be saved, saved Americans must lead the way."

Your Five Duties…

Pray that God will send a great spiritual awakening to America, that many millions of our citizens will receive Jesus Christ as Savior and Lord, and that Christians will dedicate themselves to God for spiritual living and active service within the family, the church, and the nation.

God's Promise to Heal a Repentant Nation

It is undeniable that our once great country, now mired in numerous social ills, is facing an unparalleled moral crisis. God alone holds the solution to our nation's problems—and we hold the key. The healing of our nation begins with the prayers of the saints. "If My people will humble themselves and pray, and search for Me, and turn from their wicked way, I will hear them from heaven and forgive their sins and heal their land" (2 Chronicles 7:14). We can pray in the following ways.

Pray Without Ceasing

PRAY daily that the Spirit of God will enable you, by His power, to live a godly life and introduce others to Christ as their Savior. This is the first step to good citizenship.

PRAY daily that God will change the hearts of, or remove from positions of public leadership, those officials who are godless, worldly, and disobedient to Him. Remember that godless rulership is contagious. As King Solomon said, "A wicked ruler will have wicked aides on his staff" (Proverbs 29:12).

PRAY daily that men and women of God will be elected to public office at all levels of leadership—local, state, and national—so that righteous rulership is restored. Then our land will be healed and our country will experience the abundant blessings of God. "Blessed is the nation whose God is the Lord" (Psalm 33:12).

PRAY daily "for kings and all others who are in authority over us, or are in places of high responsibility, so that we can live in peace and quietness" (1 Timothy 2:2). We may be tempted to criticize our elected officials, but praying for them is far more significant and effective. Pray that leaders will be filled with godly wisdom and stand firm for what is right and true.

To let your legislators know you are praying for them, participate in the National Day of Prayer's Adopt-A-Leader program. The Adopt-A-Leader Kit, for individual or group use, includes cards designed to encourage leaders as well as instructions on how to pray for them. You can contact the National Day of Prayer at (800) 444-8828.

After earnest prayer...

2 Register to Vote

Be registered as a qualified voter so you can practice your citizenship with accountability to God.

If You Are Not Already Registered, Do So At Once

To serve God as a citizen, you must become a regularly participating voter. But you cannot vote until you have registered your name, address, and other information with the proper authorities.

Practice Godly Stewardship

Voting is a matter of stewardship under God, yet many millions of God's people throughout America are not even registered to vote. How can we as Christian citizens expect God to restore righteous leadership through us, unless we are willing to take a few minutes to register? Only as a registered voter will you be in a position to help elect godly officials. King Solomon writes, "The good influence of godly citizens causes a city [state or nation] to prosper" (Proverbs 11:11).

Register as soon as possible so that you can vote in the next election, and in every election, as a service for God. If you are not familiar with registration procedures, call your local city or county office for information.

There may be a registration deadline several weeks before the election, so do not wait until it is too late. Voter registration forms are often readily available at post offices, libraries, or motor vehicle licensing agencies. In addition, churches are permitted by law to invite a registrar to come to the church to register people to vote.

Once you have registered to vote, join with others…

3 Become Informed

Organize and lead or participate in a study group to inform yourself and others concerning the structure of government, current political problems and issues, and how to serve God effectively in the political arena at your level of influence.

Value Knowledge

Just as the untrained soldier is at the mercy of his enemy, the uninformed Christian cannot prevail against evil forces in the world of politics. Knowledge is essential to effective action. "The wise man is crowned with knowledge" (Proverbs 14:18). To serve God effectively as a citizen, you must learn how to act for His glory within the framework of existing political processes.

How can you best begin?

Gather Information

Many sources of information are available on the political process. Numerous organizations and ministries provide summaries of current issues and updates on pending legislation. Many groups have databases you can search at their Internet website, or will send weekly or monthly updates by E-mail or fax if you request them. Newsletters, brochures, and fact sheets on specific topics can also put timely information at your fingertips.

Organize a Citizenship Group

Talk to your Christian friends about starting a study group on Christian citizenship. Invite your friends to meet with you for prayer, then explain the study group idea and show samples of the materials you have located. With the group's agreement, set a date for your first meeting and acquire the materials. Plan to meet regularly.

Begin Now

Delay can be fatal to America. Do not allow anything to hinder you from becoming a well-informed Christian citizen.

Knowledge must result in action...

4 Help Elect Godly People

Help select and elect men and women of God to public office at the local, state, and national levels. Support them faithfully throughout their terms of public service by lovingly sharing with them the biblical views on issues, praying for them, and encouraging them.

Help Restore Righteous Rule

Righteous rule brings rejoicing. "With good men in authority, the people rejoice; but with the wicked in power, they groan" (Proverbs 29:2). The most effective way to restore righteous rule and rejoicing in America is to elect godly people to positions of authority. This can be done only by informed, praying Christians like you.

How can you accomplish this?

Select a Godly Candidate

The Word of God gives us the basic qualifications of a good candidate. "Find some capable, godly, honest men who hate bribes, and...let these men be responsible to serve the people with justice at all times" (Exodus 18:21,22).

The six qualifications listed in this passage are: demonstrated capability (competence in managing business or professional affairs), godliness (spiritual maturity), honesty, integrity, industriousness, and justice. Apply these God-given standards carefully and prayerfully in selecting your candidate.

Organize a Precinct Committee

Your local political precincts are the key to victory for a godly candidate. Acquire the official precinct maps covering the district in which your candidate is running for public office. Become a precinct leader and encourage other Christians to take responsibility under God for their precincts. Enlist five to ten people to serve as a volunteer committee with each leader. Assign each volunteer to certain streets within the precinct so that all homes will be visited. Since there are only approximately 175,000 precincts in the U.S., a relatively few godly people involved at the precinct level can help to change the direction of this nation.

Move Into Action

Plan and launch precinct projects:

1. Get acquainted with the residents of each precinct.
2. Enlist additional precinct workers.
3. Update the latest official precinct lists.
4. Urge all who would vote for your candidate to register.

5. Make your candidate known by word of mouth and through literature distribution.

6. Strongly urge and, if necessary, personally assist all who favor godly candidates to vote on election day.

Your Key Role Under God

Since the key to election victory is at the precinct level, God's people can and must occupy the precincts of America as a high-priority service for Him. Five to ten dedicated Christians, each of whom spend four to five hours every month in precinct service, can usually carry their precinct for a qualified candidate who is spiritually mature. If this can be done in a majority of the precincts in your election district, your candidate will win the election.

God Will Use You

Most importantly, your precinct service will provide excellent opportunities to share God's love and forgiveness with others. As you serve God in your precinct, carry the *Four Spiritual Laws* booklets with you. Ask God to lead you to those who are ready to receive Christ. Share God's wonderful plan of salvation with them and invite them to worship God with you in your church. God wants to bless your service for Him in your precinct. You will be a blessing to others, and your own life will be enriched.

Keep Your Committee Alive

After the election, continue your precinct committee. Meet monthly for prayer and fellowship and invite others to join you. Ask God to show you new ways to serve Him in your precinct. Continue looking for and screening new candidates for various public offices at the local, state, and national levels. Keep praying, serving, witnessing, helping your neighbors, and loving others.

Finally, exercise your privileged right on election day...

5 Vote

Vote consistently in every election, after becoming informed about the various candidates and issues, and evaluating them on the basis of the Word of God.

Why You Must Vote

Only when you cast your vote do you fulfill your Christian responsibility in government. Exercise the influence that God has given you through our unique system of self-government. If you fail to vote conscientiously for godly rule, evil will increase in our nation. "When rulers are wicked, their people are too" (Proverbs 29:16). Our nation will then bear the consequences of our choices. "You will cry out for relief from the king you have chosen, and the Lord will not answer you in that day" (1 Samuel 8:18, NIV).

It is commonly believed that decisions in America are made by a majority of the people. This is not so. Decisions are made by a majority of *those who vote.* As few as 16 percent of all eligible voters in a district can elect a member of Congress. Even presidents have been elected by an average of one-half the votes per precinct nationwide.

By one vote, Texas was admitted to the Union; Hitler won leadership of the German Nazi Party; and the U.S. House of Representatives elected Thomas Jefferson as President. Your one vote does make a difference!

How can you know for whom you should vote?

Know the Candidates' Views

Make a sincere effort to obtain reliable information about all issues and candidates before casting your vote. Through your Christian citizenship group, form a Candidate Selection Committee to evaluate the various candidates and report your findings to the Christian public. Take time to attend any candidate forums held before local elections or watch televised debates in national elections.

If your congressmen and senators are running for reelection, find out how they voted on issues of critical importance to our families and our nation. Some organizations produce "Congressional Scorecards" to help you track their votes and make an informed choice at election time.

Non-partisan voter education guides can also inform you of candidates' views in presidential, congressional, state, and judicial races. Because these guides fully comply with

IRS regulations, they may be distributed in churches, despite the attempts of some to intimidate pastors from distributing them. You have a right—and a responsibility—to be fully informed before choosing those who will rule over you.

Let God's Word Be Your Guide

In making your decisions, let the Word of God be your guide. "Godliness exalts a nation" (Proverbs 14:34), so it is important to prayerfully seek God's will in all political decisions. Israel invited God's anger by selecting leaders without consulting Him: "They set up kings without my consent; they choose princes without my approval" (Hosea 8:4, NIV).

If there is no qualified candidate who is spiritually mature, vote for the one whose personal principles and platform most nearly agree with your own Christian position, based on the Bible.

Principles Are More Important Than Party

Remember that a candidate's principles are far more important than his party affiliation.

To place confidence in unworthy candidates is a miscarriage of Christian stewardship. "Putting confidence in an unreliable man is like chewing with a sore tooth, or trying to run on a broken foot" (Proverbs 25:19). Therefore, vote your Christian convictions over your party loyalty.

In 1832, founding father Noah Webster warned young people that the preservation of our government depends on their choosing righteous leaders:

"When you become entitled to exercise the right of voting for public officers, let it be impressed upon your mind that God commands you to choose for rulers just men who will rule in the fear of God. The preservation of a republican government depends on the faithful discharge of this duty; if the citizens neglect their duty and place unprincipled men in office, the government will soon be corrupted; laws will be made, not for the public good, so much as for selfish or local purposes; corrupt or incompetent men will be appointed to execute the laws; the public revenues will be squandered on unworthy men; and the rights of the citizens will be violated or discarded. If a republican government fails to secure public prosperity and happiness, it

must be because the citizens neglect the divine commands, and elect bad men to make and administer laws."

Dedication to Freedom

When the signers of the Declaration of Independence affixed their signatures to that historic document, they were well aware that if the colonial cause failed they would be executed as traitors. They were that dedicated to the cause of freedom. Any less dedication on our part will result in a loss of that precious freedom for which they and thousands of others were willing to die. We dare not fail them, ourselves, and far more important, our Lord, to whom this nation was dedicated. Our nation is now faced with its greatest crisis in history. If you ever plan to do anything for Christ and America, please do it now.